ABSURDITIES & REALITIES OF SPECIAL EDUCATION

The Best of Ants..., Flying..., and Logs

Full Color Edition

Cartoons by Michael F. Giangreco
Illustrations by Kevin Ruelle

Peytral Publications, Inc.
Minnetonka, MN 55345
952-949-8707

Publisher's Cataloging-in-Publication
(Provided by Quality Books, Inc.)

Giangreco, Michael F., 1956-
    Absurdities and realities of special education : the
best of Ants-- , Flying-- , and Logs / cartoons by
Michael F. Giangreco ; illustrations by Kevin Ruelle. --
Full color ed.
    p. cm.
    ISBN: 1890455-40-7

    1. Special education--Caricatures and cartoons.
2. Special education--Humor. 3. Inclusive education--
Caricatures and cartoons. 4. Inclusive education--
Humor.   I. Ruelle, Kevin. II. Giangreco, Michael F.,
1956- Ants in his pants. III. Giangreco, Michael F.,
1956- Flying by the seat of your pants. IV. Giangreco,
Michael F., 1956- Teaching old logs new tricks.
V. Title.

    LC3969.G519 2002   371.9'022'2
                        QBI02-200426

Library of Congress Catalog Card Number: 2002107588

Cartoon illustrations by Kevin Ruelle
Printed in the United States of America

Peytral Publications, Inc.
PO Box 1162
Minnetonka, MN 55345
952-949-8707
www.peytral.com

Contents

#	Cartoon Title	Source	
1	Fanning the Flames	Logs	13
2	Treadmill	Logs	11
3	Teaching Old Logs	Logs	9
4	Weeds or Wildflowers?	Logs	21
5	Endangered Species	Ants	56
6	Teamwork on Steroids	Ants	53
7	Workable Team Size	Flying	34
8	Marking Territory	Flying	35
9	Anatomy	Logs	3
10	Severely Dysfunctional Team	Ants	60
11	Black Hole	Logs	66
12	Roots of Special Education	Logs	68
13	Lobsterville	Ants	20
14	Extending the Continuum	Flying	4
15	Special Class Euphemisms	Logs	60
16	Placement Problem #32	Flying	31
17	Island in the Mainstream	Ants	27
18	A, B, C's of Inclusion	Ants	33
19	Snailville	Ants	13
20	Inclusion Every Tuesday & Thursday	Ants	35
21	Parole Approach	Ants	8
22	Inclusion Mishap #9	Ants	31
23	Don't Take the Bait!	Logs	64
24	Rocket Science	Ants	25
25	Swimming Lessons	Flying	20
26	Everyone is Included	Ants	30
27	Head in the Clouds	Flying	105
28	Student Relocation Program	Logs	14
29	In-Your-Face	Logs	97
30	Nth Degree	Logs	98

About the Author

Michael F. Giangreco, Ph.D., is a Research Professor at the University of Vermont (UVM). His work as a faculty member at UVM since 1988 has been on various projects with colleagues at the *Center on Disability and Community Inclusion* in the *College of Education and Social Services*. Since 1975 he has worked with children and adults with and without disabilities in a variety of capacities including camp counselor, community residence counselor, special education teacher, special education coordinator, educational consultant, university teacher, and researcher. Since 1982 he has written several research studies, book chapters, and books peratining to special education. In 1998 Michael completed his first book of cartoons, *Ants in His Pants: Absurdities and Realities of Special Education*. This was followed by two more sets of cartoons, *Flying by the Seat of Your Pants: More Absurdities and Realities of Special Education* (1999) and *Teaching Old Logs New Tricks: More Absurdities and Realities of Education* (2000). Although he will continue his more traditional writing, he also plans to continue to infuse humor into his work and find creative ways to share information about the serious issues facing people with disabilities, their families, teachers, and service providers.

About the Illustrator

Kevin Ruelle has been an illustrator in Vermont for over twenty years. Cartoons are just one of the many applications of illustration that Kevin uses in his work. He runs a successful commercial art business, *Ruelle Design and Illustration*, located in Burlington, Vermont. He and his associates produce all forms of visual communication and multimedia projects. Kevin lives with his wife Neidi and their four children, in West Bolton, Vermont.

A Word from the Author

Absurdities and Realities of Special Education: The Best of Ants...,
Flying..., and Logs (Full Color Edition) is the fourth book of cartoons I have
created with the invaluable assistance of my friend, artist, Kevin Ruelle. If
you have seen any of the first three books, *Ants in His Pants...* (1998), *Flying*
by the Seat of Your Pants..., (1999) or *Teaching Old Logs New Tricks...*
(2000), you may already know how this collaboration between Kevin and I
works. I create the original ideas, text, and sketches for each cartoon. But
since my drawing abilities have been stalled at an early third-grade level,
ever since I was in third-grade (that was in 1963), Kevin redraws my
sketches. Then we edit them until they closely reflect the ideas represented
in my original sketches. In this version we edited colors together.

The cartoons in the first three books were all in black and white. That
was a conscious decision, both for aesthetic and practical reasons. We
wanted the cartoons to be easily copied on to overhead transparencies for
display in classes, workshops, and other learning environments.

The origins of this full color edition began on Summer 2001 trip to the
UK where I had the good fortune to meet many parents, professionals and
advocates who were working to improve education for all children. Some of
them were part of a group called *ALLFIE (Alliance for Inclusive Education)*.
They requested permission to use one of my cartoons on the cover of their
magazine. What I didn't realize until the magazine arrived in the mail, was
that they had colorized the cartoon. As much as I didn't want other folks
changing the work Kevin and I did, I had to admit that it was quite nice to
see the cartoon in color. It spurred us to act -- so thanks *ALLFIE.*

The 100 cartoons included in this *"Best of ..."* collection are colorized
versions drawn from the 315 cartoons previously published in the three
earlier cartoon books, *Ants...* (1998), *Flying...* (1999) and *Logs...* (2000). The
cartoons were selected based on three primary criteria. First, we included
the cartoons that have been most frequently requested for reprinting by
advocacy organizations, parent groups, professional organizations, and
schools in their newsletters, manuals, and other resources. Secondly, my
publisher, Peggy Hammeken, always wants to make sure that there are
enough "nice" cartoons, so some of those are included. Finally, with the
limited number of slots remaining, I threw in some of my personal favorites.

As the author of several more traditional articles in professional journals and books, I have been pleasantly amazed by the power of cartoons to inform, encourage dialogue, spur action to improve education, and reduce stress by helping people smile. I have been equally intrigued by how different people respond to different cartoons. Everyone seems to have different favorites depending on their own experiences and sense of humor.

Cartoons from the early books have found their way on to the pages of many newsletters disseminated by schools, parent groups, disability advocacy organizations, and professional associations. They have appeared in books, manuals, and journals; a few were even published in a law journal. The cartoons have been used extensively as overhead projections or within learning activities in college classes, at conferences, in workshops, and at other meetings. Parents have told me they have framed cartoons that closely reflected their own experiences and hung them in their homes or offices. Other parents have used them in meetings with professionals to help get their points across. They have been given as gifts to people who "get it" and handed out as door prizes. The *Vermont Coalition for Disability Rights* used them as part of "Disability Awareness Day" at the Vermont legislature. The cartoons can be used in innumerable creative ways.

Knowing that some of you will not have seen the previous three books from which these cartoons were taken, I decided to repeat some of what I wrote before to ensure that readers have a clear understanding of my underlying thoughts and values in developing these cartoons. First, I value humor and think it is vital to our health, well-being, and creativity. Humor can also be a powerful learning tool. I wanted to address some of the serious issues of special and general education by poking fun at what we (people in the field) do. I have been challenged by the concern that some people might be offended by content that may hit a little too close to home. I have decided to take the chance that people in our field have a sufficient sense of humor to reflect on the satirical aspects of these cartoons, see the humor in them, and use them to promote better schooling. Friends and colleagues have warned me that my cartoons could be misused to promote practices that are the antithesis of what I have worked for my entire professional career. Just so there is no misunderstanding about what these cartoons stand for, I have listed here some of my beliefs related to the cartoon content.

- Individuals with disabilities are still woefully undervalued in our society.
- We waste too many of our resources testing, sorting, and labeling people, usually so we can justify serving, separating, or excluding them.
- Inclusive education is desirable; therefore, our efforts should be geared toward finding ways to make it work effectively for increasing numbers of students. Students with disabilities should have opportunities to lead "regular lives."
- Collaborative teamwork is an important element of quality education.
- Families are the cornerstone of ongoing educational planning.
- Establishing a partnership between families and school personnel is vital to quality education.
- Competent general educators can effectively teach students with disabilities when provided with appropriate supports.
- Special educators and related service providers (e.g., physical therapists, occupational therapists, speech-language pathologists, school psychologists) can, and do, make important contributions for many students with special educational needs.
- All school personnel need to work under conditions that allow them to provide appropriate education for their students (e.g., adequate staff development and inservice education, supportive supervision, reasonable caseload sizes).
- At the heart of quality education is the relationship among the members of the educational community, the quality of the curriculum, and the integrity of the instruction. We must attend to all three components if we hope to assist students in experiencing valued life outcomes.

So as you read the cartoons, keep in mind that they are meant to encourage better educational practices by highlighting various absurdities and realities of some of our current practices. I hope the cartoons stimulate you to think about things differently and that you find creative ways to use them in your own efforts to improve education for children and youth. I also hope that some of these cartoons make you smile and laugh, because we sure can use more of that in education.

Enjoy!

Michael F. Giangreco

Acknowledgments

Thanks to my colleagues, friends, and family who inspired some of these cartoons: Doug Biklen, Amanda Dana, Mary Beth Doyle, Alan Gartner, Melanie Giangreco, Michael Hock, Robert Holland, Tim Knoster, Norman Kunc, Dorothy Lipsky, Cathy Quinn, Bev Rainforth, Dan Wilkins. Thanks to Stephan Doll for his assistance in the preparation of this book and for his artistic advice. Thanks also go to Ginie Olson of *Ruelle Design and Illustration* for the input she provided during the colorizing process.
A special thanks to Peggy and Roberto Hammeken of *Peytral Publications* for their continued willingness to support the development of these cartoons as an avenue for learning. My most special thanks goes to my fun and funny family, my wife Mary Beth and my children, Dan and Melanie, for their ongoing encouragement even when they thought the cartoons were the ultimate in corny.

FANNING THE FLAMES OF CHANGE:
LIGHTING A FIRE UNDER PEOPLE WITHOUT
BURNING YOUR BRIDGES

THE TREADMILL OF CHANGE

KNOWING HOW HARD IT IS TO EFFECT
MEANINGFUL CHANGE IN PEOPLE,
MR. MOODY DECIDES TO
WORK HIS WAY UP TO IT BY
TEACHING OLD LOGS NEW TRICKS.

WHAT DO YOU CHOOSE TO SEE?
WEEDS OR WILDFLOWERS?

HERB AND SALLY ADD THE ELUSIVE
"COLLABORATIVE TEAM" TO THEIR
LIFE LIST OF RARE
AND ENDANGERED SPECIES.

IN AN EFFORT TO MAINTAIN A
WORKABLE TEAM SIZE, MR. MOODY
SUGGESTS LIMITING MEMBERSHIP TO
THE NUMBER OF PEOPLE THAT
CAN FIT IN A PHONE BOOTH.

MARKING THEIR TERRITORY
TEAM MEMBERS IN EXPERIMENTAL THERAPY LEARN TO OVERCOME PRIMITIVE BEHAVIOR.

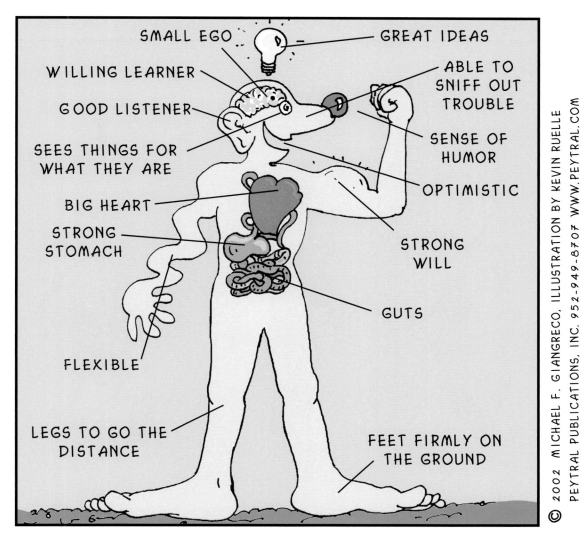

ANATOMY OF AN EFFECTIVE TEAM MEMBER

SEVERELY DYSFUNCTIONAL TEAM

BOLDLY NOT GOING WHERE TOO MANY
OTHERS HAVE GONE BEFORE!

RITA RETURNS TO DIG UP THE
ROOTS OF SPECIAL EDUCATION.

MR. CRUSTY WELCOMES FRED TO THE
LOBSTERVILLE SPECIAL EDUCATION
CENTER WHERE THEIR MOTTO IS
"YOU CAN GET IN, BUT YOU CAN'T GET OUT!"

EXTENDING THE CONTINUUM: WHERE WILL IT END?!!

STUDENTS WHO MISBEHAVED IN A SPECIAL ED SCHOOL ARE TRANSFERRED TO A MORE RESTRICTIVE PLACEMENT.

OPENING THE DOOR ON
SPECIAL CLASS EUPHEMISMS

PLACEMENT PROBLEM #32:
FUNCTIONING LEVEL RATHER THAN
CHRONOLOGICAL AGE.

© 2002 MICHAEL F. GIANGRECO. ILLUSTRATION BY KEVIN RUELLE
PEYTRAL PUBLICATIONS, INC. 952-949-8707 WWW.PEYTRAL.COM

ISLAND IN THE MAINSTREAM

MRS. JONES AND MRS. COOPER ARE
STILL TRYING TO FIGURE OUT WHY FRED
DOESN'T FEEL LIKE PART OF THE CLASS.

© 2002 MICHAEL F. GIANGRECO. ILLUSTRATION BY KEVIN RUELLE
PEYTRAL PUBLICATIONS, INC. 952-949-8707 WWW.PEYTRAL.COM

THE ABC'S OF INCLUSION

ADMINISTRATORS AT
SNAILVILLE SCHOOL LAMENT
THE SPEED OF CHANGE.

PRINCIPAL JONES FAILS TO RECOGNIZE THE CONTRADICTION IN TERMS.

"PAROLE APPROACH"
TO SCHOOL INCLUSION

INCLUSION MISHAP #9: DUE TO A FAULTY INTERCOM, MRS. SNIPPETT THOUGHT THE PRINCIPAL SAID, "YOU HAVE A NEW STUDENT COMING TO YOUR CLASSROOM - HE HAS DISABILITIES. DO YOUR BEST TO *ELUDE* HIM."

AVOID THE TRAPS OF QUASI-INCLUSION:
DON'T TAKE THE BAIT!

FRANK LEARNS THAT INCLUSION DOESN'T
HAVE TO BE ROCKET SCIENCE.

THE EVOLUTION OF SWIMMING LESSONS: SURPRISINGLY SIMILAR TO THE EVOLUTION OF INCLUDING STUDENTS WITH DISABILITIES IN GENERAL EDUCATION.

INCLUSIVE EDUCATION
BECOMES A MOOT POINT

INCLUSIVE EDUCATION:

PROVING YOU CAN DREAM WITH YOUR
HEAD IN THE CLOUDS AND STILL HAVE
YOUR FEET FIRMLY ON THE GROUND.

TO ADDRESS THE LINGERING STIGMA OF DISABILITY LABELING, MR. MOODY IMPLEMENTS THE DISTRICT'S NEW "STUDENT RELOCATION PROGRAM."

JUDY'S BRAND OF
"IN-YOUR-FACE"
SELF-ADVOCACY FIRST SHOWED
ITSELF AT AN EARLY AGE.

PETER PONDERS OVER APPAREL TO WEAR
TO HIS NEXT IEP MEETING.

DISABILITY LINGO
GOES TO CAMP!

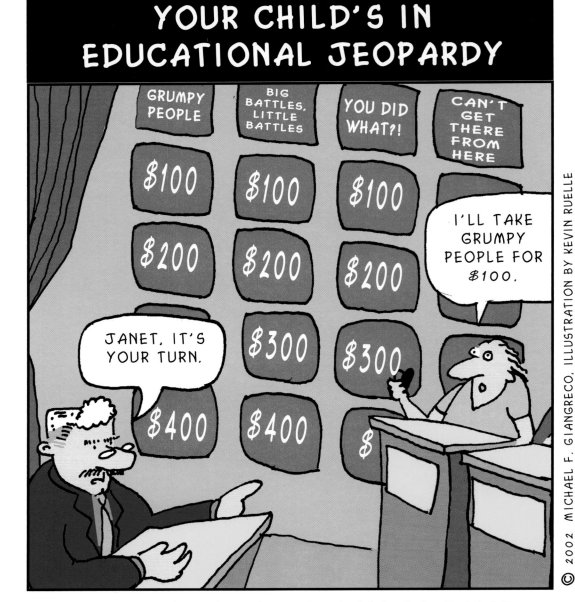

PARENTS FIND NEW WAYS TO RAISE
MONEY FOR EDUCATIONALLY RELATED
LEGAL FEES.

A DISTANT COUSIN OF PINOCCHIO
DISCOVERS HE HAS INHERITED ONE OF
HIS FAMILY'S RECESSIVE TRAITS.

MR. GREEN PREPARES FOR HIS
CHILD'S IEP MEETING

OUTNUMBERED?

HAVING SUFFERED THROUGH EXCESSIVE
EXPOSURE TO PROFESSIONALS, PARENTS
LOOK FOR FUN WAYS OF COPING.

HOME PROGRAMMING
COLLIDES WITH
HOME REALITY!

DUE PROCESS

THE GAME WHERE EVERYBODY GETS A TURN, NOBODY HAS FUN, AND EVEN IF YOU WIN, YOU FEEL LIKE YOU'VE LOST!

DESPERATE PARENTS RESORT TO
ESTABLISHING THEIR OWN
"FREQUENT INCLUDER PROGRAM."

MRS. HOPE FOUND THAT SOME OF HER BEST INSTRUCTORS WERE STILL IN SECOND GRADE.

PEERS
RESORT
TO
SUBVERSIVE
TACTICS

MYSTERIES OF FRIENDSHIP.

PURPOSEFUL
EDUCATIONAL
ACCOMMODATIONS
CREATING
EXCELLENCE

ADJUSTMENT PROBLEMS:
USUALLY THE ADULTS,
RARELY THE KIDS.

ED IS DIAGNOSED WITH MULTIPLE
PERSONALITY DISORDER.

THEATRE OF THE ABSURD

LEGISLATIVE PRACTICAL JOKES

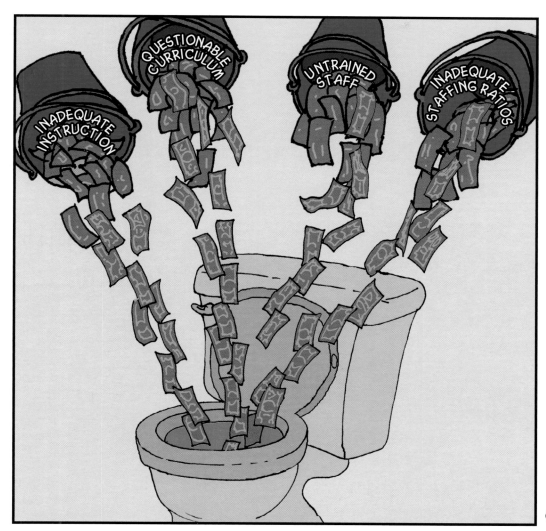

UNLESS YOU SPEND ENOUGH MONEY
TO MEET A BASIC
THRESHOLD OF EFFECTIVENESS,
YOU MIGHT AS WELL JUST FLUSH IT!

SCHOOL ADMINISTRATORS OFTEN FIND
THEMSELVES BETWEEN
A ROCK AND A HARD PLACE.

NO DUMPING!

NATURAL SUPPORTS BREATHE;
WHEN USED APPROPRIATELY, THEY MAKE THINGS FEEL MORE COMFORTABLE.

LABORATORY RETRIEVER

SUPPORT SERVICES THAT ARE
"ONLY AS SPECIAL AS NECESSARY"
FIT JUST RIGHT!

UNEMPLOYED ACTORS ARE RECRUITED
TO FILL THE NATIONAL
TEACHER SHORTAGE.

STUDENTS CONDUCT A SCIENTIFICALLY
CONTROLLED EXPERIMENT TO VERIFY
THAT TEACHERS REALLY DO HAVE
EYES IN THE BACK OF THEIR HEADS.

SIMPLE ACCOMMODATIONS
IN THE AGE OF LITIGATION

SCHOOLS ADOPT CONSUMER
EVALUATION TECHNIQUES
FROM INDUSTRY.

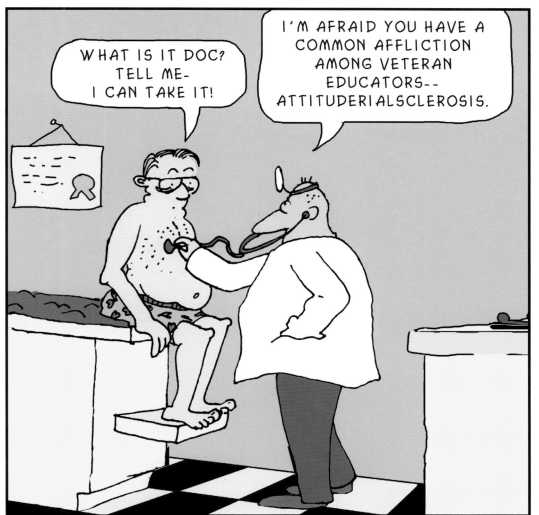

HARRY IS DIAGNOSED WITH
HARDENING OF THE ATTITUDES.

AFTER TRYING TO FLY BY THE SEAT OF HIS PANTS, FRED LEARNED THAT GOOD TEACHING REQUIRES GOOD PLANNING.

GENERATING AND EVALUATING
IDEAS SIMULTANEOUSLY IS LIKE
TRYING TO RIDE A BIKE BY
PEDALING WITH THE BRAKES ON.

THE LEAD BALLOONS
OF SPECIAL EDUCATION.

LARGE CASELOADS FOR SPECIAL EDUCATORS:
THE NUMBERS JUST DON'T ADD UP!

INDIVIDUALIZED EDUCATION:
MRS. SMITHFIELD FAILS TO NOTICE
THE CONTRADICTION.

TEAMMATES ENGAGE IN THEIR ANNUAL
POST-IEP COMPLETION RITUAL.

PARAEDUCATOR ISSUES:
JUST THE TIP OF THE ICEBERG

© 2002 MICHAEL F. GIANGRECO, ILLUSTRATION BY KEVIN RUELLE PEYTRAL PUBLICATIONS, INC. 952-949-8707 WWW.PEYTRAL.COM

GUARDIAN ANGEL

SUPER-MAGNET

STUCK LIKE GLUE

HOVERCRAFT

HELPING OR HOVERING?

JOEY NOTICED A MYSTERIOUS FORCE FIELD
AROUND HIS ASSISTANT THAT CHILDREN
COULD NOT BREAK THROUGH.

SCHOOL LUNCH
ATROCITIES

THE SHADOW KNOWS:

RODNEY'S SUSPICIONS WERE
ACCURATE. UNBEKNOWNST TO HIM,
A PARAPROFESSIONAL HAD BEEN
ASSIGNED TO BE HIS SHADOW.

BAND-AID APPROACH:
ARE WE EXPECTING TOO MUCH
OF INSTRUCTIONAL ASSISTANTS?

THE OLD MEDICAL MODEL

STAIR WARS

FREDDIE IS NOT AMUSED BY HIS PHYSICAL
THERAPIST'S CHOICE OF HALLOWEEN
COSTUME.

ADVENTURES IN ZIPPING
ZONE OF PROXIMAL CONFUSION

ONLY IN A PHYSICAL
THERAPIST'S DREAM.

THE INTERSECTION WHERE DIETING
AND REHABILITATION MEET.

SHOPPING AROUND:
DO YOU KNOW THESE PEOPLE?
THEY NEVER MET A THERAPY
THEY DIDN'T LIKE.

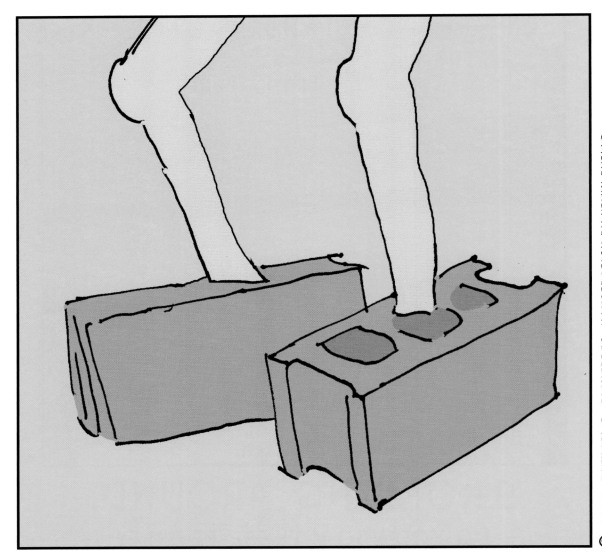

A FORMER GANGSTER TURNED THERAPIST
RELIES ON OLD SKILLS IN DEVELOPING HIS
EXPERIMENTAL "CEMENT SHOE THERAPY."

AFTER MONTHS OF PSYCHOTHERAPY,
SYLVIA RETRIEVES REPRESSED
CHILDHOOD MEMORIES OF THERAPEUTIC
POSITIONING THAT EXPLAIN HER SHOE
FETISH IN ADULTHOOD.

SYLVIA CONTINUALLY STRUGGLES TO UNDERSTAND THE DIFFERENCES BETWEEN THE DISCIPLINES.

"WE HAVE WAYS OF MAKING YOU TALK!"

ALL OF THE DISTRICT'S SCHOOL PSYCHOLOGISTS ARE SUPPLIED WITH EQUIPMENT TO CARRY OUT THEIR TWO MOST COMMON FUNCTIONS.

THE #1 SIGN A TEACHER DOES NOT FIND A CONSULTANT'S INPUT SUPPORTIVE:

CONSULTANT'S REPORT IS FOUND SHREDDED AS BEDDING FOR THE CLASSROOM HAMSTER.

WHO WILL WANT TO DO THESE JOBS
WHEN THEY GROW UP?

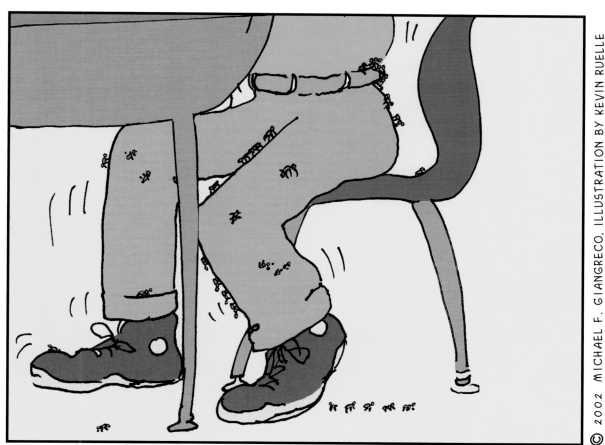

AFTER A HASTY SPECIAL EDUCATION
PLACEMENT FOR BEHAVIOR PROBLEMS,
SCHOOL OFFICIALS WERE EMBARRASSED
TO LEARN THAT MARTY REALLY DID HAVE
ANTS IN HIS PANTS.

LITTLE SHOP OF HORRORS

CONSIDERING HER STUDENTS WITHOUT
DISABILITIES, MRS. BAKER
REALIZES DAVID'S UNUSUAL
BEHAVIORS AREN'T THAT UNUSUAL.

REMEMBER,
THIS IS ONLY A TEST!

CONFUSED BY A STATE EDUCATION DIRECTIVE, MR. MOODY ARRANGES FOR EVERY STUDENT IN HIS SCHOOL TO MEET THE STANDARDS.

DESPERATE MEASURES

HOW MANY STUDENTS ARE FALLING
THROUGH THE CRACKS?

THE THREE MUSKETEERS
OF GOOD PRACTICE:
VALUES, LOGIC, AND RESEARCH
(IN THAT ORDER).

FAULTY RESEARCH LOGIC

ODD JOBS!

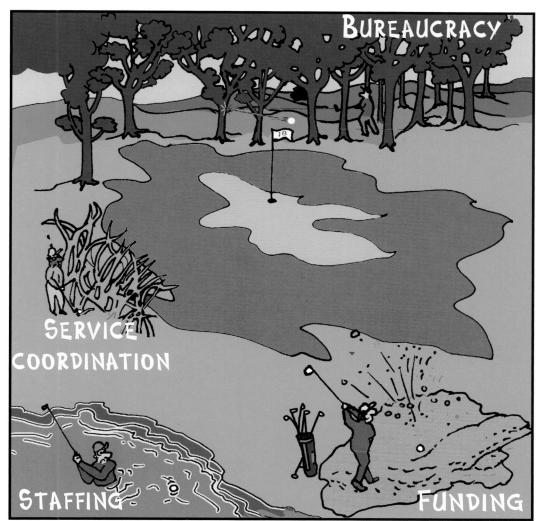

THE HAZARDS
OF TRANSITION PLANNING
ARE PAR FOR THE COURSE.

VEGAS CASINOS BUCKLE UNDER POLITICAL PRESSURE TO STOP STEREOTYPING DISABILITY CHARACTERISTICS AS CRIMINAL BY INVENTING THE TWO-ARMED BANDIT.

SUPPORTED EMPLOYMENT LESSON #6:
GIVE A PERSON A FISH AND THAT
PERSON EATS FOR A DAY. TEACH A
PERSON TO **WORK** AND THAT PERSON
CAN BUY A FISH ANY DAY!

COUNTER INTELLIGENCE

FOLLOWING FIERCE FIGURING AND
FORMULATING, FERN FINDS THE COMMON
DENOMINATOR OF QUALITY EDUCATION.

CLEARING A PATH
FOR PEOPLE WITH SPECIAL NEEDS
CLEARS THE PATH FOR EVERYONE!

Additional Staff Development Cartoon Books!

Ants in His Pants:
Absurdities and Realities of Special Education
1998 Edition   1-890455-42-3

Flying by the Seat of Your Pants:
More Absurdities and Realities of Special Education
1999 Edition   1-890455-41-5

Teaching Old Logs New Tricks:
More Absurdities and Realities of Education
2000 Edition   1-890455-43-1

Absurdities and Realities of Special Education:
The Best of Ants…, Flying…, and Logs.   Full Color Edition
2002 Edition   1-890455-40-7

Full Color Note Cards – Set A and Set B
Each boxed set includes: 16 full color note cards with envelopes (8 different designs).
Note cards are blank inside.   Great for personal use or a unique gift!

If you have questions, would like to request a catalog, or place an order, please contact *Peytral Publications, Inc.* We will be happy to help you.

Peytral Publications, Inc.
PO Box 1162
Minnetonka, MN   55345-0162

Questions: (952) 949-8707
Order line: 877-PEYTRAL (877-739-8725)
FAX: (952) 906-9777

Or visit us online at:
www.peytral.com